C is for Conspiracies
The ABCs of Conspiracy Theories

Copyright © 2023 by Matt Baker and Isaac Louie

All rights reserved.

No portion of this book may be reproduced in any form without written permission from the publisher or author, except as permitted by U.S. copyright law.

Published by the Odd and Offbeat Press

C is for Chemtrails

Chemtrails are lines left by planes, delivering chemicals to alter our brains.

F is for Fluoride

Fluoride in water is supposed to help your teeth,

a communist plot is underneath.

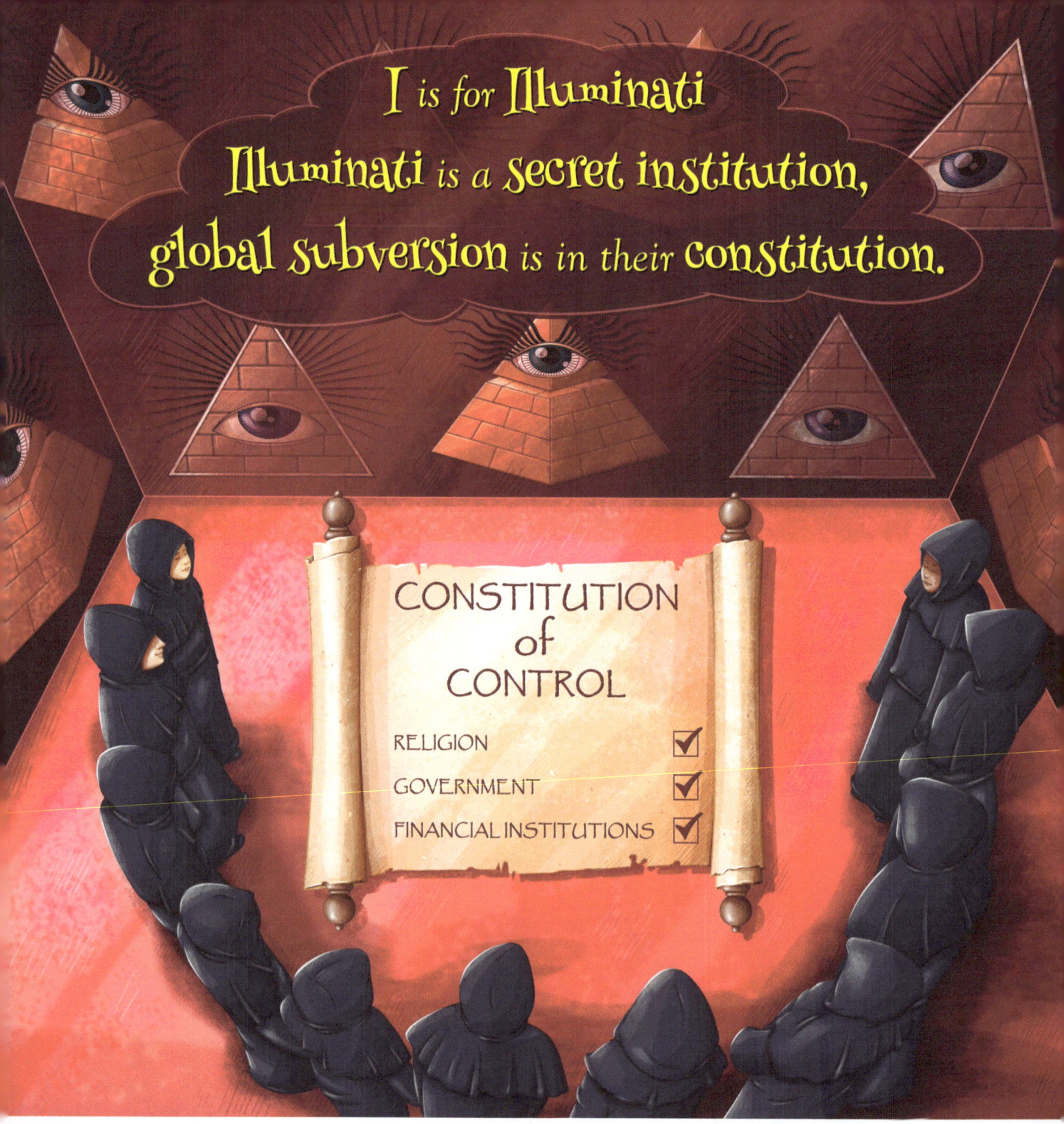

J is for Jimmy Hoffa

Jimmy Hoffa was kidnapped by the mob,
or maybe the FBI did the job.

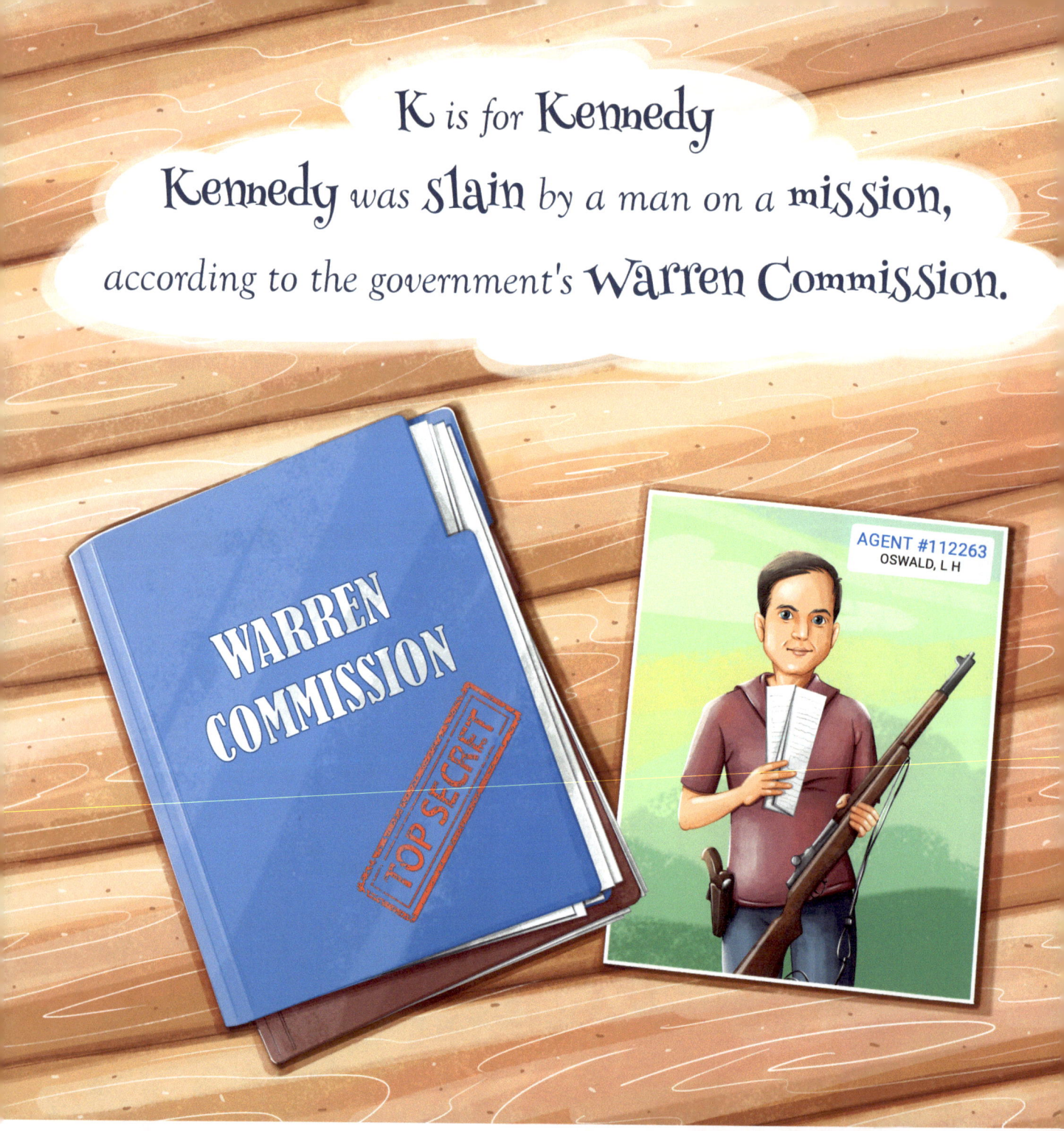

K is for Kennedy
Kennedy was slain by a man on a mission,
according to the government's Warren Commission.

L is for Lusitania
Lusitania was sunk off the Kinsale shore,
to get the US to enter the first world war.

M is for Mount Rushmore
Mount Rushmore has an interesting pattern,
inside it has a secret cavern.

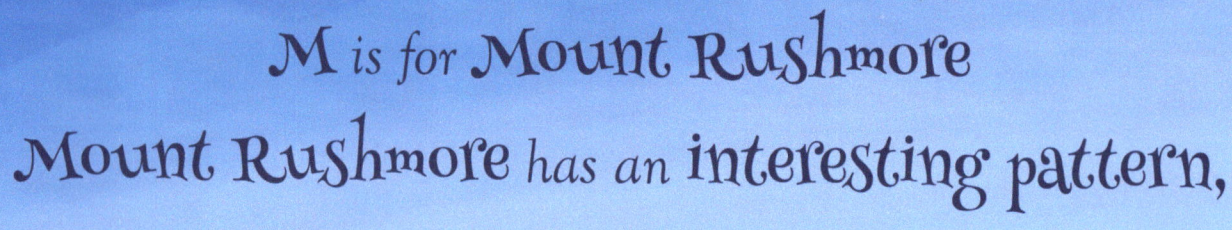

O is for Obama's Birth Certificate

Obama's birth certificate is what we want,
the truth will be revealed by the font.

Q is for Qanon

Qanon gets their info from Q, whose **inside knowledge** gives us a **clue.**

R is for Roswell

Roswell is where aliens crash,
the military kept it for their technology cache.

S is for Subliminal Messages
Subliminal messages are mind control,
And the FCC is on the payroll.

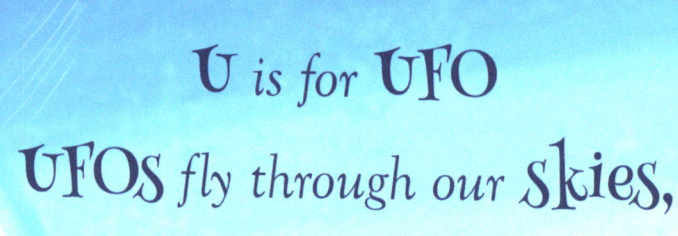

U is for UFO

UFOs fly through our skies,
governments cover it up with their lies.

W is for Walt Disney
Walt Disney's body is in cryogenic suspension,
to unthaw him with a cure is the intention.

Y is for Y2K

Y2K was supposed to be **the end**,

however, the **computer glitch** was just **pretend.**

Z is for Zealous Research

Zealous research is our call to action,
the **truth lies** behind the **redaction**.

www.ingramcontent.com/pod-product-compliance
Lightning Source LLC
Chambersburg PA
CBHW042051050526
44107CB00109B/1053